MW01228216

Forty Years –
a Celebration

The Mississippi Poetry Society

South Branch

Forty Years – A Celebration

From The Mississippi Poetry Society South Branch

www.misspoetry.net

Copyright 2023 © Doctor's Dreams Publishing,
www.Doctors-Dreams.com

All rights to the poems within reside with the authors, who have graciously shared them for your enjoyment. Please respect those rights.

No part of this publication may be reproduced, stored in a retrieval system, or transmitted in any form or by any means, including photocopying, recording, or other electronic or mechanical methods without the prior written permission of the editor.

Manufactured in the United States of America

ISBN: 978-1-942181-33-0

Table of Contents

Welcome.. 1

President's Message 3

Past President's Message... 5

Eunice D. Barnes.. 7

   If I Could by Eunice Barnes 7

Patricia Butkovich 8

   April This Year Found Me...by Patty Butkovich 8

   Celebrating our Flag, an Acrostic by Patty Butkovich........... 9

   Beads and Moonpies by Patty Butkovich............................ 10

   A Favorite Four-legged Friend by Patty Butkovich 11

   Better Than Santa by Patty Butkovich 12

   Gingerbread! by Patty Butkovich 13

Cecile B. Clement.. 14

   Liberated Blooms by Cecile B. Clement 14

Bert Corwin 15

   Ripples by Bert Corwin 15

Laura Gabrielle Cupps.. 16

   Finally Celebrating Myself by Laura Gabrielle Cupps 16

   These Special Moments by Laura Gabrielle Cupps 17

Judy Davies 18

   Artistry by Judy Davies 18

   Cat-egorically Speaking by Judy Davies............................. 20

   Grandma's Legacy by Judy Davies..................................... 21

   Christmas Angels by Judy Davies 22

Oh, Oh – It's Christmas by Judy Davies 23

Old Friends at Christmas by Judy Davies 24

Rebuilding Christmas Traditions by Judy Davies 25

Brenda Brown Finnegan 26

Haiku by Brenda Brown Finnegan 26

On Turning 80 by Brenda Brown Finnegan 27

Road Trip by Brenda Brown Finnegan 27

Eating My Way Through Ireland by Brenda Brown Finnegan
.... 28

Frog on the Windowsill by Brenda Brown Finnegan 30

On Entering College at Age 33 by Brenda Brown Finnegan 30

Our Christmas Heritage* by Brenda Brown Finnegan 31

Helen Jarvis 32

St. Ann's Chapel by Helen Jarvis 32

Mary Beth Magee 33

Editorial Comment by Mary Beth Magee 33

Plans by Mary Beth Magee 34

The Diehard Fan by Mary Beth Magee 35

Gum by Mary Beth Magee 36

Angels in My Life by Mary Beth Magee 37

Christmas Shopping by Mary Beth Magee 38

Elaine McDermott 39

Eve's Side of the Story by Elaine McDermott 39

Spirit of Marie Laveau by Elaine McDermott 40

Monita McLemore 41

Along the Shore by Monita McLemore 41

Taming the Wild Heart by Monita McLemore...................... 42

Eva Voncile Ros... 43

Madam Chairman's Ghost by Voncile Ros......................... 43

We Dream by Voncile Ros.. 45

Mary Lee Terry.. 46

Fall by Mary Lee Terry 46

Grands Matter by Mary Lee Terry 46

My Friend's House by Mary Lee Terry................................ 47

The Mardi Gras Parade by Mary Lee Terry 48

Marguerite Watkins.. 49

Misplaced Efforts by Marguerite Watkins 49

South Branch Group Poems 50

Pandemics   (written 9-15-20)... 51

Hurricanes   (written 9-23-20).. 51

Autumn Escape   (written 9-30-20)..................................... 52

Trick or Treat   (written 10-10-20)...................................... 53

October Moons   (written 10-23-20) 54

Jack O Lantern   (written 10-31-20).................................... 55

Veteran's Day   (written 11-12-20) 56

Thanksgiving   (written 12-1-20) 57

December Days   (Written 12-18-20)................................... 58

Happy New Year   (written 1-9-21)..................................... 59

Cooperative Sonnet - January 2021 (written 1-20-21).......... 60

A Valentine Sonnet   (written 2-18-21)............................... 62

St. Patrick's Day   (written 3-18-21)................................... 63

My Mother Always Told Me   (written 5-12-21)................. 64

Celebrating America's Birthday   (written 6-28-21)............ 66

Summertime, 2021   (written 8-9-21)................................. 67

It's Fall Y'all   (written 10-4-21)... 68

Awesome Autumn   (written 11-30-21) 69

Mississippi Poetry Society - South Branch Poets of the Year.. 71

Former members of MPS South Branch.................................. 73

Mississippi Poetry Society History 75

Welcome

Welcome to our poetry party! In this volume, we seek to honor our past, celebrate our present and look forward to our future. Our branch of the Mississippi Poetry Society is not the oldest, but we are a vibrant group.

You will find verses from some of the members we have lost over the years as well as the work of our current members. Each verse is a precious glimpse of the poet's heart.

The poems are organized in alphabetical order by the poet's name. No ranking is implied.

May you enjoy reading them as much as we enjoyed writing them.

President's Message

It's such an honor to be chosen as president of the South Branch. I am so proud of my outstanding board and look forward to an exciting year. Several young people have joined, and we will be hosting the 2023 MPS Spring Festival in April, as well as producing this South Branch 40th Anniversary Anthology. We are looking forward to bigger and better things and a busy poetry year.

Mary Lee Terry
Ocean Springs, MS
2022-2023 South Branch President

Past President's Message

Since I served as the South Branch president from September 2016 – September 2022, I've been asked to write a message for this 40th Celebration Anthology.

It has been an eventful 5 years since our last anthology with Judy Davies and Brenda Finnegan dominating the competition for South Branch Poet of the Year. Both also went on to win the Poet of the Year title at the state level, and to publish their chapbooks, *Inkspirations* (Judy) and *Horn Island Vista* (Brenda).

Covid 19 kept us isolated in our homes several years but when we began meeting again, we named Mary Lee Terry, South Branch Poet of the Year and we also elected her to serve as our current president.

Even though we could not continue meeting in the Gautier Library during the many long months of the pandemic, we remained active via email. You will find a section in this anthology that contains the group poems composed by South Branch. We started an email poem with a title and passed it around with each person adding a line or two. It was fun to see each poem grow, and it kept us in touch. I think our completed poems came together to make some interesting poetry.

We hosted the state poetry festival at Gulf Hills in 2018. It required lots of work and donations from each member. The Friday evening get together was a great success and enjoyed by all as we shared a poem about our alter ego and dressed the part to add to the fun. Winner of the competition by unanimous consent was our current president, Mary Lee Terry. She revealed to us that her alter ego was to be Queen of England.

Dr. Sue Brannon Walker, the Stokes Distinguished Professor (Emerita) of Creative Writing at the University of South Alabama, Publisher/Editor of Negative Capability Press, Poet Laureate of Alabama from 2003-2012, and author of 15 published collections of poetry was our featured speaker. Her morning workshop was titled: "Language is Not Set Like Concrete: It's Taffy: The Matter of Revision" and the address after the evening meal at McElroy's: "Honoring Your Why to Live: Your Life – Your Legacy."

The contest results were announced, and winning poems read. South Branch poets claimed our share of the prizes with Judy Davies getting the top 'Best of the Fest' honor. We will be hosting the state festival again on April 21-23, 2023, at the Walter Anderson Museum in Ocean Springs, MS.

South Branch monthly meetings were filled with several guest speakers and many members who gave us programs to improve our writing and increase our knowledge of famous poets.

South Branch members always spend time at each meeting with a read around. Some of those poems are printed on the following pages for your enjoyment.

With gratitude and deep appreciation to each member for all you have contributed,

Patty Butkovich
South Branch Past President

Eunice D. Barnes

If I Could by Eunice Barnes

If I could
I would
curl a rainbow
round every rain-soaked mountain peak;
bind every broken heart
with taut, tough cord.
Invite every child to ride, ride, ride
on painted carousel.

If I could
I would
lure a winging bird
into every green-boughed, budding tree;
make every summer dream
come true;
capture all beautiful things
for my poem.

If I could
I would
paint every face
with the glow of health
and put Easter
in everyone's soul.

Second prize
1979 Mississippi Poetry Journal Contest Issue

Patricia Butkovich

April This Year Found Me…by Patty Butkovich

with extra mail in the mailbox
beautiful, funny, and heartfelt cards
bountiful birthday posts online
bouquets of flowers and lunches with friends.

I pray more than I did in the past
I am spending more time in The Word
I attend weekday mass more often
and volunteer wherever I can.

I hitch up the sweatpants, tie the Nikes,
then trudge all around the neighborhood.
Each year my pace is a little slower
the distance growing a little shorter.

I'm cooking less, napping more.
taking time to smell my roses
  (when they finally bloom again).
I love watching my birds and squirrels
as they dine on the seeds I provide.

My heart's filled with joy.
my soul with His peace
I feel that I'm planted
where He wants me to be.

Celebrating our Flag, an Acrostic by Patty Butkovich

First summer of the Civil War
Legend says Flag Day was celebrated
At Hartford, Connecticut, in 1861.
Glory to the red, white and blue

Declaration of Independence was about one year old
At the birth of our U.S. flag
Yet it flies today to unite us as one

Just as we celebrate our nation's birthday on the fourth of
        July
Unfurl the flag on June 14th and celebrate its birthday.
Never forget the military who defend this USA
Ever in peace and war, the flag speaks freedom

14th of June is the day to fly Old Glory proudly!

Beads and Moonpies by Patty Butkovich

Patchwork quilt of people
casual, costumed, debonair
jolly, stolid, painted faces
packed along the thoroughfare.

Musical mélange of songs
converging on the ear
beads, doubloons and Moonpies soar
raining through the atmosphere.

Mermaids swim in waves of foil
glittered boat is packed with krewe
octopi in deep sea chambers
pirate's treasure chest to view.

King and Queen survey their realm
from a float with gilded throne
dazzling satin sequined guise
champagne toasts to set the tone.

The patchwork's now a solid blanket
of arms outstretched. Solicitors.
Shining toothy faces calling,
"Throw me somethin', Mister!"

A Favorite Four-legged Friend by Patty Butkovich

In my dusty vault of memories
from my childhood on the farm
I recall those of Harry the horse,
named for Harry S. Truman who had
a sign on his desk that read:
The buck stops here.
This horse had tried to buck my dad off
the day that we got him, so the name, Harry.
Though he was a bit high spirited
Harry was always gentle around me.
I'd stick a carrot in my pocket
when I took him his bucket of oats.
Harry liked his oats, but he loved the carrot.
He'd nibble at my jeans until he found
his treat, then flip his head and give
a little whinny. I swear he had
a twinkle of triumph in his eye.
Harry was my all-time favorite
pet and companion during
my early years.

Better Than Santa by Patty Butkovich

To Nicholas, the wonder worker Saint,
Friend and protector of children.
They desperately need you,
To work your mighty deeds.

To orphans of the AIDS epidemic,
Send some food and clothing.
To the street children in Latin America,
Send a place to lay their heads.
To China's sweatshop children,
Send time for them to go to school.
For Indian children sold into slavery,
Grant them freedom.
To many American children
Instead of things, send a firm hand of love and guidance
St. Nicholas, this Christmas, please…a miracle.

Gingerbread! by Patty Butkovich

Her December tradition is gingerbread.

Gingerbread houses of all sizes and shapes.

They have delighted her children and now her grands,

Plus the students lucky enough to be in her class.

Also the shut-ins, and of course, nursing home residents.

She has, no doubt, baked thousands of gingerbread boys

And hundreds of walls and roofs for the houses.

Her December kitchen must be filled to the brim

With sticky white frosting for snow,

M&Ms for the shingles,

Gumdrops for the doorknobs,

Marshmallow snowmen,

Starlight mint steppingstones

And an array of other candies.

Much to the delight of all who know her,

My friend, Ellen.

Cecile B. Clement

Liberated Blooms by Cecile B. Clement

The garden blooms have been set free, at last,
From binding rows and tiring pruning acts.
For time and time man kept them in a cast
Of charted circles, boxes, and abstracts.

The man devised the scheme of bloom and seeds
To beautify his house and please his soul.
He fought to keep the snails and wicked weeds
At bay – the plants were trained to play their role.

The flooding winds have forced the house to fall
And sent the man to seek a safe repose.
At last emancipation came to all –
The daring daisy and the fragrant rose.

It seemed that freedom from the binds was breath,
But cost was dear, and numbers fell to death.

Bert Corwin

Ripples by Bert Corwin

Ages pass, and people come and go,
Imprisoned in an increment of time.
Some minutes are used wisely, others lost,
Return no more to offer a reprieve.

We stretch our minds to understand the "why."
We ask our doctors to postpone the "when."
We mind not our beginning come so late,
Regret our ending will appear so soon.

We walk beside a tranquil lake and plunge
A hand into the water's cool embrace.
We pull it out and ripples spread around.
We wait, and all is as it was before.

We dare not think that this describes our lives,
That we can be begotten, then forgotten.
The ripples we send out will never die,
But we choose if they hurt or help mankind.

So speaks Ecclesiastes, "generations
All pass away and others take their place."
But ripples are like bread upon the waters
Recovered often after many years.

They represent the things we have done
The good, the bad, the sad parts and the fun.

Category Third Place Winner
MPS Journal Spring Contest Issue 1997

Laura Gabrielle Cupps

Finally Celebrating Myself by Laura Gabrielle Cupps

She's reminded of her body and its many imperfections
Every time she opens her phone full of actresses and
models
This spurs her urge to grab and throw some bottles
While she decides what of her figure to cut in sections

Lost in this endless view of hatred of her reflections
The envy and despair halt rising, and she dawdles.
A new urge now arises and herself she now coddles
Her view of herself then transforms to replace her
predilection.

Love and acceptance are showering and overwhelming her.
Her body screams out a "thanks" because it waited
So many years for this moment to finally have transpired.

Now that it happened, the girl no longer a self-saboteur,
More moments of happiness to come were fated
Because she had realized she too deserved to be admired

These Special Moments by Laura Gabrielle Cupps

Here comes that special time of year
In which we all come and gather together
With those that we hold near and dear
No matter the kind of weather.

The day has been filled with preparing
For guests from far and wide to arrive
Who spent all morning deciding what they're wearing.
Once they arrive, everyone begins to feel alive.

There are glasses and dish-ware that clink
As meals made with love feed us well
The evening comes and goes in a blink
Leaving us with memories on which to dwell

It makes one ponder why we wait
To see each other until another special date

Judy Davies

Artistry by Judy Davies

An intricate pen and ink drawing hangs in our entrance hall;
it defines our home as welcoming to artists one and all.
The canvas is always ready, the mission always clear,
an atmosphere for creativity is allowed to flourish here.

Precision and patience work magic in clay and in stone.
Potters fashion their clay; sculptors chip away the unknown.
The artist is poised with his brush in hand,
"Bring the canvas to life" is his internal command.

The composer refines sound using ear and electronics,
stringing together pitch sets, notes and harmonics.
Sensitive creativity and originality he must release
providing the framework for each masterpiece.

Dancers develop poise in body with purposefulness,
from plié to pointe, the embodiment of gracefulness.
Dancing with abandon, each performance flawless,
speaking through motion, the epitome of artfulness.

Through prose and poetry the writer's feelings are heard
as he hones his craft of the written word.
Drawing in his reader, giving voice through technique,
with spirit and soul his art form must speak.

Whether captured in clay, on canvas or in stone,
via music, dance or simply words alone,
the creative process brings new life to our health
when we hunger for culture, not just monetary wealth.

Each form of artistry plays a critical part,
each displays vision through its own brand of art.
Absence of the arts points us down a black hole.
The essence of art is it enriches the soul.

*Dancing Poetry Festival Grand Prize Winner 2014,
"Artistry," with music by Judy's composer husband,
Ken Davies, was danced on stage by Natica and
Richard Angilly's Poetic Dance Theater Company,
then toured throughout California. The Dancing
Poetry Competition is sponsored by Artists Embassy
International. "Artistry" was the winner of the 2009
Senior Poet Laureate title for Mississippi and has also
been featured by United Poets Laureate International*

.

Cat-egorically Speaking by Judy Davies

Golden eyes, soft black fur;
I'm Midnight, a beautiful black cat.
Do you think I get any respect? Heck, no!
For example, when I was young I always
had the last place on the broom on Halloween.

Fur goodness sake, we'd fly around for what seemed
like hours. If I'd fallen off on a fast turn, I doubt
I'd have even been missed. But when I was just a kitten,
I got to fly on a whisk broom. My young mistress and
I fit snugly together, just the two of us. Now that was fun!

The head witch of our coven has two huge cats that fly with
her. Neither one is black. Talk about discrimination!
They must really hang on tight because she is powerful.
She flies a vacuum cleaner— newest model with "attachments."
Yep, a pair of reflective-collared fat cats.

Now I don't mean to get my fur in a fluff, but I think I deserve
equal standing. At our last "catversation" we voted for equality.
My current ride isn't too bad, and I don't mind working my way
up to a better broom; but if I could nail a spot on that vacuum
cleaner, well; it would be pure purr–fection!

Grandma's Legacy by Judy Davies

Hair pulled back, knitting needles flying,
we read the patterns to her as her eyesight failed.
No one could knit faster or more accurately.
She seldom missed a stitch, even at age 92.

Colorful scarves and mittens emerged like Christmas
magic; intricately detailed sweaters a special prize.
My daughter has the baby sweater grandma knit for
her first great-great-grand— kittens playing with yarn.

Knitting was her exquisite talent. But, my most
unforgettable Christmas gift came when I was 14.
No longer able to see, she passed to me her legacy:
her journals—78 years of family history, essays
and poetry she'd begun when she was 14.

Christmas Angels by Judy Davies

It's a cold winter's night in Harlem.
Dirty urchins play in the street amidst the reality
of store front glitz and stove pipes painted
red and white to replicate candy canes.
Factory smoke covers the sky like a gray blanket,
the only blanket these families can afford.

But that night the "North Pole Express" drops onto a roof.
You can tell that it's real by each pawing hoof.
Santa's pack is crammed full, nearly bursting at the seams
provided by those who know what Christmas really means.

These are the angels who give gifts of food, clothes,
toys and basic family needs. They are the ones who
allow each of us time to be thankful for all that we have.
These are the angels who are the true spirit of Christmas.

Oh, Oh – It's Christmas by Judy Davies

Once upon a Christmastime
I thought that it would be just fine
if I ignored the winter weather,
and skipped Christmas all together.

I didn't put up a Christmas tree,
remembering the trouble it could be.
I didn't decorate the house
or buy the cat a Christmas mouse.

But I found my thoughts were quite amiss;
Christmas isn't that easy to dismiss.
I've changed my mind; I'm so behind,
Christmas shopping needs a mastermind.

Now all I want for Christmas is an extra month to shop,
hoping I'll finish the job before I just plain drop.
I've bought cards, gifts, bows and paper
in hopes I can complete this caper.

I've learned my lesson, have no fear.
When I think of Christmastime next year
I won't allow my plans to go awry;
I'll begin my shopping in July!

Old Friends at Christmas by Judy Davies

Here am I with my pen in hand
Watching snowflakes fall like grains of sand,
Recalling nights watching movies at the Grand,
As I write old friends at Christmas.

How we braved those wintry winds each night,
Tried to shelter noses from frostbite,
Strolled house to house to see the Christmas lights,
So I write old friends at Christmas.

Stopping in the small town square café,
Pushing the troubles of the world away,
Sipping hot chocolate with whipped cream;
We were young then, with so much time to dream.

Years gone by, now we're miles apart.
At Christmastime those past reflections start.
So many thoughts still warm my heart,
As I write old friends at Christmas.

Remembering, old friends at Christmas.

*Music for Old Friends at Christmas was composed
by Judy's husband, Ken. The CD was recorded by
David Delk. It is available thru ken@kendavies.net.*

Rebuilding Christmas Traditions by Judy Davies

It's time to recall the season that was canceled in the
17th century, re-invented two centuries later in America,
and was changed from a raucous carnival holiday to a
family-centered day of nostalgia and peace.

Sadly, the materialism, media, advertising and
mass marketing have taken much of the joy out
of Christmas. Let us celebrate the blended
customs that make each family's Christmas unique.

Celebrate traditions under a canopy of twinkling lights,
stroll past colorfully lit homes, rouse to the ring of
church bells in the distance or duck into a shop for a little
extra-special Christmas shopping or a box of Christmas
sweets.

Escape to a quieter time when Victorian carolers sang
and Santa always had time for one more picture.
Delight in the season and the loved ones who surround you.
Now is the time to fashion your own Christmas traditions.

Brenda Brown Finnegan

Haiku by Brenda Brown Finnegan

Sun through Mason jars:
tomatoes, green beans, peppers-
a kaleidoscope.

(2020)

*This poem was inspired at an art/poetry show at the Mary C. Cultural
Center in Ocean Springs by the painting of "Kaleidoscope of
Vegetables" by local artist, Pat Bernstein, as well as the poems from
Gertrude Smith's upcoming poetry book:* **Kaleidoscope, Worlds
Beyond My Window.** *(Gertrude was a poet and artist, and a member
of MPS until her death.) This haiku won 2nd place in the Traditional
Haiku Award - National Federation of State Poetry Societies in 2020. It
is published in* **Encore.**

Leaves fall on packed sand;
slab left by the hurricane
is hidden, waiting.

(2005)

The first hint of Spring:
humming, buzzing in the air-
tiny hummingbird.
(4/20/21)

On Turning 80 by Brenda Brown Finnegan

The nice party at Mary Mahoney's
with our immediate family:
underneath the majestic canopies
of a massive 2,000 year old tree.

Gifts, balloons, champagne, and glitter were spread
along the table in Lucien's Room;
with lovely aromas of fresh baked bread,
and a crystal vase of roses in bloom.

Having all our three children present
and my husband of almost sixty years
made a pleasurable evening and meant
so much to me that I cried happy tears.

(While under a 2,000 year old tree,
eighty doesn't seem quite that old to me!)

Road Trip by Brenda Brown Finnegan

Four old girls each pack separately;
then one sunshiny Fall morning
cram their suitcases, pillows,
and ice chests full of wine,
apples, yogurt, and cookies,
leaving behind husbands,
grown children,
grandchildren's schedules,
weekly church obligations,
and head out to leaf peep
along the back roads
of yellow and orange;
for their annual adventure.

Eating My Way Through Ireland by Brenda Brown Finnegan

In Galway, I had fish and chips
Two pubs in Newbridge filled my lips
With soup and sandwich, good and hot
Then salmon, grilled in Glendalough.
On the island of Inishsheer,
I said, "No," to Guinness beer,
But Bailey's coffee warmed me up
And then I had a second cup
With salmon salad and brown bread
That Irish food went to my head.
The Plaza's M'issippi Mud cake
Was the best I ever ate!
My slacks were tight at old Killarney
Yet lunch was great at Castle Blarney.
In Limerick, 'twas Irish stew;
The hotel meals were "cordon bleu."
In Kilkenny, we shopped and ate:
Lunch at a pub; a sandwich plate.
Walking in the chilly rain,
We stopped for Bailey's once again.
Popped in for supper at Miller's Pub;
We had to have some good, hot grub:
Mussels, prawns and more fried chips
(What was that threat? "A minute on the lips?")
Our final dinner at Newpark Hotel
A five-course meal; dessert, as well.
Lunch in the airport once again
While we waited to board the plane.

Laden down with souvenirs
And pounds we gained while over there.
The plane groaned as it left the ground
But now we're back in our hometown.
The scales squealed "Yikes" as I got on,
But now I'm back - dieting, and home.

*Published in **Boyne Berries 5**, Spring 2009,*
Trim, Co. Meath, Ireland

Frog on the Windowsill by Brenda Brown Finnegan

Rhinestoned blue-eyed frog
Glitters and winks whenever I dust
My daughter's windowsill.

One day I'll gaze too deeply
Into that shiny blue
And fall into the brightness,

Slowly tumbling,
Twirling into nothingness,
Dissolving into the light.

On Entering College at Age 33 by Brenda Brown Finnegan

A college cafeteria is a lonely place
When you're the only one there
Whose name you know.

And more than tables separate
You from the young
In tee-shirts and faded jeans.

Our Christmas Heritage* by Brenda Brown Finnegan

Years ago, my mother decided to share
her large collection of Christmas dishware.
I had several pieces of the same design
so she decided to pool hers with mine.

My brother and his wife had Pfaltzgraff, too,
but, solid white, without the Christmas hue
that included a green tree and a tiny train
rolling around a little village's terrain.

She decided to split her dishes between us,
and brought boxes of plates, saucers and cups,
a large platter, tureen and several bowls
to our Christmas party (and some hot rolls).

Since I expected only half of her dishware
I asked my brother if they got their share.
He said he hadn't received a single cup
or a plate or saucer from which to sup.

Realizing that Mother was confused
with early dementia, and, bemused
we sorted her set in more or less half
hugged and thanked her and had a good laugh.

Now, she, my brother and his wife are deceased,
so when I set the table for our Christmas feast,
I remember them all, and through my tears,
cherish the tradition we shared through the years.

*The Pfaltzgraff pattern is "Christmas Heritage"

Helen Jarvis

St. Ann's Chapel by Helen Jarvis

A small wooden chapel in the fork
of a winding country road.
Memories of Easter Mondays, school holidays,
an Easter Egg Hunt
Carrying a brown bag lunch.
Riding on the school bus, simple days,
the good 'ole days.
Our Parish mission, St. Ann's Chapel,
Many years have passed.
So I wondered as I visited, a small country church.
Sacred Heart, Dedeaux, not much bigger
that the missions, as I recalled.
Wondering is that Chapel still at
Claremont, VA?
Is it forgotten, by the side of the road,
The fence all grown over with honeysuckle vines?
Not so, Dedeaux, I've been told about its
humble beginning.
Hoping with love and much prayers this
county church will serve for a long time,
Sacred Heart, Dedeaux, MS

Mary Beth Magee

Editorial Comment by Mary Beth Magee

I watched the pages as she turned them,
And wished I could read her mind
As easily as she read the words.
Did she like what she saw?
Did my efforts please her?

No glimmer of expression crossed her face
As she worked her way
Through my hard work.
The days of writing,
More days of rewriting.

My heart – poured out in each line –
Carried a flood of hopes
And dreams and prayers
From my mind to the page,
Now to her eyes.

Would she be touched by what I'd written?
Would the phrases she saw there offend her?
Or would she recognize intent
And see the message tucked away
Behind the fiction I described?

She read on, eyes moving to and fro,
Otherwise a sculpture in flesh,
A part of the chair in which she sat.
My mind raced in fear,
Prepared for icy disapproval.

At last, she raised her head.
Her tear-glazed gaze met mine,
"I didn't know," she whispered.
"You never said anything before.
Why didn't you tell me how you felt?"

Plans by Mary Beth Magee

My best laid plans, so careful made,
Fall down in harsh reality's face.
Intentions cannot overcome
The anchor-drag of commonplace.

The daily jobs demand my thoughts
And fill my time with minor tasks.
The calendar and clock run on,
No care for boons my poor heart asks.

So, time moves on and passes by.
"Tomorrow" is my mantra bold,
Unpromised and then unfulfilled.
Today is gone, yesterday cold.

We will catch up, we promised sure.
A fishing trip or camp out scene
Would give us all the time we need
To share our thoughts and quiet dreams.

Then death, which overrules all time,
Steps in and takes a loved one's hand.
In shambles lie those well-intentioned
Thoughts of acts I might have planned.

"I should have" and "I wish I had"
Accuse me of my fallen schemes.
To say "I love you" one more time
Would be an answer to my dreams.

I laid my plans but failed to act.
The things I meant to do, undone
Until too late. Now grief wells up,
And sadness blocks the brightest sun.

Farewell, dear one. Forgive me, please.
I loved you and I always will.
Until the day we meet again,
Within my heart I hold you, still.

Previously published in The Tunica Voice

The Diehard Fan by Mary Beth Magee

Were you listening last night? Did you hear the cries?
Did you feel the anguish in the desperate sighs?
Was your heart torn out by the end result?
Did you take the conclusion as awful insult?
When the winner was named, did you shed a sad tear?
Does the outlook seem grim for the rest of the year?
Had you poured your heart into supporting your team?
Has the final score punctured your bubble of dream?
Don't let the bad news make you lose hope or pride.
Believe in them, cheer them and stay for the ride.
For any game's outcome can go either way.
Watch us beat the socks off them the next time we play!

Category First Place Winner
MPS Journal 2022 Contest Issue

Gum by Mary Beth Magee

I didn't mean to drop my gum.
I wanted just to chew it.
But sometimes gum don't listen good
And it just had to do it.
It jumped itself right out my mouth
And hit the floor, ker-splat.
And Susie stepped right on it.
Can you imagine that?
Now you know why it is there
And why my sister's crying.
I told you that it's my fault.
There ain't no use in lying.
But like I said before, I really
Didn't <u>want</u> to do it.
I didn't mean to drop my gum.
I wanted just to chew it!

Angels in My Life by Mary Beth Magee

An angel crossed my path today.
I don't think that he knew
I recognized his humble guise
Or that his heart shone through.

He offered help when I had need,
Asked nothing for his care.
Went on his way, but left a smile
Behind. Now, if I dare

I hope to serve as someone else's
Angel in disguise.
To be God's hands to one in need,
To serve as His supplies.

God gives so much to all of us.
His bounties overflow.
May I serve as a conduit
That others His love know.

Christmas Shopping by Mary Beth Magee

I start my Christmas shopping on Dec. 26th.
My purchases I gently store away.
No rush of frantic shopping sprees or rushing to the mall
Will mar my celebrating Christmas Day.

My list is kept in secret, doublechecked and finely tuned.
I aim to meet each Christmas giving need
With thoughtful gifts bought wisely at a sale price in good
    time.
No Scrooge am I – now that you must concede.

The Christmas spirit lasts me all year long, and that's my
    plan,
My loved ones always forefront in my heart.
It's not about the shopping, but the people on my list.
Best wishes are the things which fill my cart.

I'm always Christmas shopping, if the honest truth be
    known.
Sometimes I may forget which gifts I've bought.
But a Baby in a manger is the reason for the day.
That love is center most within my thoughts.

Elaine McDermott

Eve's Side of the Story by Elaine McDermott

"Bone of my bone,
flesh of my flesh,"
that's all I hear from Adam.
I know I'm made of bone;
he forgets he's made of mud.
Then Adam reminds me that God
made him first, and he
named all the animals.
He gets angry if I call a lion
a leopard.

I can't remember all the names,
but I do remember one: snake!
He told me I would know all things
if I ate the apple, the forbidden fruit.
I took a bite and it was good.
Afraid God would be angry,
I gave Adam a bite, too.

Well, God was angry, so Adam
blamed it all on me. I blamed
that snake, but we were expelled
from the garden. Now here we are
wandering somewhere east of Eden,
wearing those animal skins
Adam named. And it's all his fault.

Spirit of Marie Laveau by Elaine McDermott

It's whispered on a starless night
that when the fog rolls in,
Marie Laveau's seen in the streets,
a woman wild with gin.

She had a lover long ago,
who proved to be untrue;
she made a doll that looked like him,
and practiced her voodoo.

At the Silver Slipper Palace,
a chorus girl named Belle
longed for Marie's dark-skinned Creole
and placed him in her spell.

Marie then made a man of clay;
she dressed him bold and smart.
She found a sharp and silver pin
and stabbed him in the heart.

He died that night in young Belle's arms.
Marie went mad with pain.
She made a doll that looked like Belle;
she found her pin again.

It's whispered on a stormy night
that above the thunders din,
Marie is heard out in the streets
repenting of her sin.

Monita McLemore

Along the Shore by Monita McLemore

O' all the gifts bestowed upon mankind,
A beach just has to be among the best.
For sheer variety, you'll never find
More riches for your mind and soul's arrest.

The ever-changing scenes from day to day...
Each season finds no shoreline quite the same.
Surprises greet you all along the bay,
Delighting; and you're happy that you came.

A bold sunset of shades you'd not believe,
A seashell of a kind not often found,
The graceful flight of gulls that dip and weave
And playful dolphins feeding in the sound.

　　　One cannot walk barefoot along a shore
　　　And not return much richer than before.

Category First Place Winner
MPS Journal Spring Contest Issue 1997

Taming the Wild Heart by Monita McLemore

Each time I hear the wild geese overhead
I stop what I am doing just to stare.
I daydream of the land they're headed for
and yearn to join them on their journey there.

My senses overflow at such a scene...
The moon has framed them in a silhouette...
Their patient rhythm winging beckons me
to follow, soar above earth's closing net.

A scent of burning leaves hangs in the air
to sting my nostrils, turn my thoughts around;
a sound of distant mumbling train wheels hum
against unwilling ears to force me down.

For I would fly this moment if I could
to all the unknown places far away.
Though circumstance has clipped my wings for now,
This wanderlust will bloom another day.

Category Third Place Winner
MPS Journal Spring Contest Issue 1997

Eva Voncile Ros

Madam Chairman's Ghost by Voncile Ros

One day as Madam Chairman
Rose to have her say
She just quietly and publicly
Fainted dead away.

Now anyone can tell you,
If they've been around at all
This was clearly out of order,
Most improper protocol.

The agenda had proceeded
To the very last report,
But alas, poor Madam Chairman
Had an uncooperative heart.

The ladies asked each other
Exactly what they should do
Being out of order
Was something entirely new.

So, one by one they took their leave
Quite clearly in dismay.
They walked out quietly,
Not knowing what to say.

Now people say that Madam Chairman
Haunts their meeting place,
And that every single member
Claims to have seen her face.

They claim to see her pointing
To the agenda in her hand.
They've tried and tried, but still
They cannot understand.

For Madam Chairman will not rest,
Her ghost will still return
Until the ladies realize
They never did adjourn!

Previously published in Pieces of Silver
Mississippi Poetry Society South Branch
25th Anniversary Anthology

We Dream by Voncile Ros

We dream of angels floating by
While snow white clouds swirl in the sky.
We dream of lily pads of luxury;
Of perfect worlds for you and me.
We wish upon a star
While gazing from afar
And ride a sparkling moon beam to the end.
We laugh as we descend.
When we awake to eat our cake
Our snow white clouds have vanished with the wind.
We cannot see the moonbeam,
Yet, we can dream.
We dream, and dare to reach out for the star.
We know it's there – we've seen it from afar.

Mary Lee Terry

Fall by Mary Lee Terry

Falling leaves of yellow, red, brown and gold
Always bring on a sight to behold.
Leaves for the children to romp in and play,
Leaves that have to be raked up every day.

Grands Matter by Mary Lee Terry

Grandchildren are God's greatest invention,
But great-grandchildren speak even louder.
There is something that says I can't be prouder.
Spending time with them is my intention.

They may be at times so noisy and loud.
Life loses its meaning as you grow old.
Death looms its ugly head that seems so cold.
Time spent with these children makes me so proud.

The shuffle I came with is almost gone.
This old boy seems to have much more life.
Wondering what happened to all my strife,
You then realize this is where you belong

I'm now eighty-nine and I can't believe,
The great-grandchildren are now my reprieve.

My Friend's House by Mary Lee Terry

I drove to my friend's house
leaving traffic noise behind.
The quiet was oh, so deafening
but the peace I felt was mine.

She met me at her new home
built on her former land.
The first home nature had destroyed.
The new one, made with helping hands.

We got to tour the house;
the view was so serene
that I could see the hand of God
as I looked out through the screen.

The house front faced the water
Horn Island could be seen
The birds, the flora, and the view
showed God's creation so keen.

The front porch wrapped around the house;
the windows showed the view
of God's handiwork in front of it
and the Gulf of Mexico, too.

We all enjoyed the lunch,
read poems that we all shared,
spoke of the blessings of our Lord-
His promise showed he cared.

As I walked down the stairs,
and bid her spouse goodbye,
saw twelve seagulls fly by
as I looked up to the sky.

As I quietly drove away
I thought, "Could disaster strike another day?"
But, just as the phoenix rose again
Her faith said, "Come what may."

The Mardi Gras Parade by Mary Lee Terry

That one day we went to the Mardi Gras parade,
I looked for a place where there was some shade.
My granddaughter was a three-year-old child.
The people were friendly, but a bit wild.
The beads flowed freely from all of the floats.
She would catch a bead and then she would gloat.
The revelers' energy that day was quite high
Astride each float as they all passed by.
One of the riders threw a doubloon on the land
Reaching down, a small foot stepped onto my hand!
My granddaughter grinned but her foot stayed
That day we went to the Mardi Gras parade.

Marguerite Watkins

Misplaced Efforts by Marguerite Watkins

"Where are the children?" brought no running child
To greet Aunt Lyra calling through the door--
The children spoke respectfully and smiled,

Returned to reading where they were enisled
Like Crusoe in the mysteries of lore--
"Where are the children?" brought no running child,

Therefore determined Lyra appeared riled,
When twins, Leanne and Lee hugged distance more.
The children spoke respectfully and smiled.

Though Lyra's visits, like clockwork, selfstyled,
Set arrowed hands with hope that she would score.
"Where are the children?" brought no running child.

And Mama took her to the kitchen, whiled
Away some time with Lyra…years before
The children spoke respectfully and smiled.

Aunt Lyra had become unreconciled
To stillborn twins that caused her to implore…
"Where are the children?" not their auntie's child,
The children spoke respectfully and smiled.

Category Second Place Winner
MPS Journal Spring Contest Issue 1997

South Branch Group Poems

During the COVID-19 pandemic, our branch did not meet regularly but we did write! We wrote themed verses by email.

Once a theme was selected, participating members were assigned a turn to post to the project. With individual members adding lines or couplets to a verse on a particular topic, we created South Branch Group Poems. These verses sometimes took a day or two, sometimes longer depending on members' schedules. They were always fun to read as they grew with each contribution.

Celebrate with us the spirit of prevailing over adversity as you enjoy these group-generated verses.

Pandemics   (written 9-15-20)

Panorama of life changes in 2020.   (Patty)
Alone, hiding from an unseen enemy.   (Joan)
Needing to see my family and friends again.   (Barbara)
Daily I pray a vaccine be found.   (Mary Lee)
Endless stressors, faceless behind masks,   (Judy)
Masks that hide the pain of isolation   (Brenda)
Illuminating our need for human interaction;   (Faith)
Confident a vaccine for the virus will be found. (Elaine)
Slowly creeping back to normality.   (Rob)

Hurricanes   (written 9-23-20)

Hanging on every word from the Weather Channel
    (Brenda)
Urgent messages from family and friends   (Faith)
Rushing to purchase water and food (Barbara)
Really terrified of storms, glued to weather channel (Joan)
Incorrigible waters infiltrate every perforation (Patty)
Crescendo crashing consuming currents creating caustic
    catastrophe (Phillip)
Alighting from the heavens, intent on destruction (Robert)
Names assigned from Greek alphabet for the first time
    since 2005 (Elaine)
Ever grateful for God's love, even in the storm (Mary Beth)
Since the storm has passed, it's now time for the clean-up
    (Mary Lee)

Autumn Escape   (written 9-30-20)

Arriving at an Autumn Escape (Barbara)
Up atop a mountain dressed in multicolored glory, almost
    Heaven at my fingertips (Joan)
The fields are alive, delicate to behold (Judy)
Under heaven, the time has come for season's turning to flame.
    (Mary Beth)
Migrating birds flash color in the sky (Phillip)
Nights become cooler; an autumn moon rises (Brenda)

Ephemeral transitions playing the heart's strings, holding the
    soul captive (Robert)
Swaying leaves of red, yellow, brown and gold blaze across the
    horizon (Mary Lee)
Carving pumpkins, eating s'mores, falling leaves, falling temps
    make a perfect fall night (Betty)
All nature is overflowing, beautiful and bountiful (Elaine)
Partake a breath of October's crisp, cool air (Patty)
Escaping at last, the endless humidity and heat of summer. (Patty
    for Faith)

52

Trick or Treat   (written 10-10-20)

Tints of yellow and orange from the canopies fall (Robert)
Rowdy ragamuffins, rusty robots, and randy rangers roam
    the roads (Phillip)
In a pumpkin head container go goodies, treats and candy
    (Mary Lee)
Can children's teeth survive the ghoulish onslaught of
    sweets? (Mary Beth)
Kids in colorful costumes knock on neighbor's doors,
    pumpkin bags in hand for treats (Judy)

Our little munchkins, their overstuffed bags in tow, scurry
    through the neighborhood (Joan)
Ringing bells, demanding candy, a covey of witches
    invades me (Elaine)

Though this year's celebration is different, quieter, due to
    the pandemic...(Brenda)
Racing home, pint-sized goblins gorge on their goodies
    (Betty)
Eagerly sorting through their treasures for the favorite
    treats. (Barbara)
Alternative activities will be the 2020 agenda (Patty)
Thoughts of past Halloweens haunting our dreams. (Faith)

October Moons   (written 10-23-20)

October full moon shines through porch rail cracks
    over the dark concrete floor, like train tracks. (Brenda)
Clouds are illuminated in the moonlight of the night sky
    creating spooky images as they slowly drift by.
    (Barbara)
Trees stand like sentinels in the quiet of the night
    throwing odd shadows in silver moonlight. (Faith)
Once in a Blue Moon, or so the story goes,
    October's moon shines so brightly, maybe it glows
    (Betty)
Blue moon, rare phenomenon, and rarely blue
    Why are we so fascinated by you? (Joan)
Eerie second moon, a Halloween trick to my eyes,
    the first moon now past, the second a mask in disguise.
    (Judy)
Rare and precious, a month with two.
    What does a blue moon say to you?   (Mary Beth)

Mighty gusts twirl orange leaves,
    fall colors a palette weaves (Philip)
Over the sky the dark clouds roll,
    Enthralling the mind, immersing the soul. (Robert)
October moonbeams dancing in the trees,
    Orange and gold leaves swaying in the breeze. (Elaine)
Nights turn to magic when there's a Blue Moon
    Now is the time for young lovers to spoon. (Mary Lee)
Since the 2020 Blue Moon won't make you swoon,
    Step out of your cocoon, look up and commune. (Patty)

Jack O Lantern   (written 10-31-20)

Just as I pulled into the driveway, I saw someone running off
    with my pumpkin. (Elaine)
At least I THINK it was a "someone." (Faith)
Curses!! My grandson grew that pumpkin and proudly
    presented it to me to carve. Who steals a pumpkin anyhow?
    (Joan)
Knowing who that scoundrel was who absconded with my prize
    pumpkin, I began to plan sweet revenge. (Betty)

Oh, just wait until that thief comes back and picks up the "new"
    pumpkin on my front steps!! (Brenda)

Letting that thief steal that pumpkin will be my sweet revenge!
    (Barbara)
And now, I'm off to Home Depot to get a few supplies. (Patty)
Naughty, naughty! Nothing like a nighttime nosey no-goodnik
    nabbing neighborhood needs! (Judy)
Trickers tumbling on tawdy torrential trails. (Phillip)
Exempt from decency's law, he thinks he is. He is not! (Mary
    Beth)
Round the corner I peered, waiting for him to pilfer my pumpkin
    full of exploding chocolate. (Robert)
Nit Nuts know that thievery does not pay. Now we all made it a
    poem anyway. (Mary Lee)

Veteran's Day   (written 11-12-20)

Vicissitudes of life, or just desire to serve is the drive.
    (Robert)
Every generation has sacrificially served to ensure our
    freedom. (Betty)
The news came, you have been drafted to serve in Vietnam,
    a conflict that America should have never been in.
    (Mary Lee)
Every veteran is a hero and we owe a debt of gratitude to
    each for the freedom we enjoy. (Joan)
Recognizing these heroes is honorable but will never be
    enough. (Faith)
Acting on our behalf, they picked up arms in defense of our
    freedom and liberty, from the Revolutionary War until
    today.   (Brenda)
Noble men and women served our country with honor and
    valor. (Barbara)
Sacrificing life and limb for all Americans. (Patty)

Dedicated to duty, diligent and determined, proud to serve.
    (Phillip)
Any day and every day should be a day to honor those who
    serve, past, present, and future. (Mary Beth)
Young and old, they rallied to the call. Let freedom ring!
    (Elaine)

Thanksgiving   (written 12-1-20)

Thanksgiving Day is America's pride. (Mary Lee)
Having family and friends by our side. (Barbara)
All eagerly await Macy's balloon parade. (Elaine)
Now we can anticipate the scrumptious dinner our families
     have made. (Betty)
Kranberries, green beans, and marshmallow yams, (Phillip)
Some broccoli casserole and honey baked hams (Robert)
God's many blessings at the forefront this day, (Faith)
Inviting our guests to bow heads and pray. (Brenda)
Veterans stationed away join us for this special meal.
(Judy)
I hope, sharing our holiday, their loneliness begins to heal.
     (Joan)
No matter the menu, the main course is love. (Mary Beth)
Grateful Americans give thanks to our God above. (Patty)

December Days   (Written 12-18-20)

Decking the house with holly and lights (Philip)
Eating lots of holiday delights (Barbara)
Carousing at a distance, family in the heart (Robert)
Every good wish for those nearby and far apart (Betty)
Masked and social distanced where'er we go (Patty)
Being hopeful, star gazing, and wishing for snow! (Brenda)
Each year Christmas brings new beginnings (Mary Lee)
Ringing in the season has my head spinning (Elaine)

Don't forget the Savior, the heart of the season (Mary Beth)
And may your faith increase beyond all earthly reason
     (Faith)
Yuletide carols with cups of warm cider, a favorite festivity
     (Judy)
Soon, we place the baby Jesus in the manger under the tree
     and thus, we complete the nativity.   (Joan)

Happy New Year   (written 1-9-21)

Having a party's a no-no this year. (Patty)
And getting the COVID is what we all fear. (Barbara)
Put the New Year at the top of the list. (Mary Lee)
Poetry from us all, just give it a new twist! (Judy)
You ring out the old...thank goodness it's gone. (Philip)

Needing a safer future in 2021. (Brenda)
Ever looking forward to brighter days, (Robert)
When just being with others won't fail to amaze. (Faith)

Year ends, new year begins with promise and hope (Elaine)
Even in the chaotic times, we just have to cope. (Betty)
Although last year was dark, 2021 promises light. (Joan)
Redeemed by courage, faith and hope bright. (Mary Beth)

Cooperative Sonnet - January 2021 (written 1-20-21)

(This is a cooperative sonnet. Each person contributed a line for the three quatrains and then all added an ending. Pick the one you like best.)

Shakespeare is the model for me and you (Mary Lee)
The beauty of his sonnets will not fade (Barbara)
Though written old, they read as new (Philip)
Of love, of life, his art through words displayed (Judy)

A snowy path around an icy pond (Joan)
Icicles hanging from the roof like spears. (Betty)
As if a dream from out the Great Beyond (Robert)
Memories of winters in younger years (Brenda)

Camellias bloom, the winter's precious rose (Patty)
A rose by any other name is twice as sweet (Elaine)
Love's fragrance fills the heart as well as nose (Mary Beth)
And stokes cold embers into fiery heat. (Faith)

(Here are the endings.)

Although January's winters can be rough
We look forward to an early Spring. Enough. (Betty)

So read his sonnets on a winter's day
Then go outside to walk briskly and play (Barbara)

Before the vestiges of winter die
April is peeking through a sapphire sky (Elaine)

Inspired by the Bard we work our art
And hope our words will find a waiting heart (Mary Beth)

Through winter's storms we use Will's sonnet form,
Write our poems and long for love so warm (Patty)

As waves mingle with the heart's shore
We find spring permeates our hearts once more (Rob)

Words can be powerful for poets like you
Shakspearean sonnets are always new (Mary Lee)

Almost any subject you wish will do
Now write a lovely sonnet to please you (Joan)

A month of unrest; a month to ponder
And new beginnings; a time of wonder (Brenda)

Touching messages speak with words sublime
A welcome nod to joy of Shakespeare's rhyme (Judy)

A Valentine Sonnet   (written 2-18-21)

Tree branches sway in a rhythm of love. (Judy)
The pretty birds chirp a romantic song. (Barbara)
And I'm as happy as a turtle dove. (Elaine)
Riding on cloud 9 as I sail along. (Joan)

My love will soon be coming home to me. (Patty)
Everyone's a lover on Valentine's Day. (Betty)
I fall in love with everything I see. (Mary Beth)
Candy, cards and flowers are on display. (Philip)

Shant love come more oft than once in a year? (Caleb)
Red roses and chocolates bring romance (Mary Lee)
Ringing love's bells in heart, in soul, and ear (Rob)
My love holds me spellbound in Cupid's trance. (Faith)

Remembering the joys of heart days past (Brenda)
I pray this Valentine's won't be our last. (Brenda)

St. Patrick's Day   (written 3-18-21)

Although he was not Irish, he became (Brenda)
a lucky devil in his soul and heart (Faith)
And on the Emerald Isle, to his acclaim (Rob)
Jesus Christ became known by what he taught. (Mary Lee)

Paddie ran off the serpents from the isle. (Caleb)
It was a miracle for all to see. (Philip)
He shared Christ with every man, woman, child. (Mary Beth)
A green shamrock represents One in Three. (Betty)

Parades, Irish dancing, music abound. (Judy)
Plenty Corned Beef, Cabbage, Green Beer for all. (Joan)
Not one sober Irishman can be found. (Elaine)
"Raise a toast to St. Patrick!" is their call. (Barbara)

Throw ancestry away, wear green and play (Patty)
Everyone is Irish on St. Pat's Day. (Patty)

My Mother Always Told Me   (written 5-12-21)

My mother told me more by what she did.
Deeds of love showed more than the things she said. (Barbara)

Never look a gift horse in the mouth.
If you do, all your fortunes will go south! (Betty)

Never wear ragged, holey underwear.
If you're in a wreck, you'll go to ER care. (Patty)

It is the height of rudeness to be late.
Be known as one who's early for the date. (Joan)

Do your homework first and do not delay.
Otherwise, you will have no time for play. (Judy)

My mother always told me to be good,
and be a lady, as she said I should. (Mary Beth)

This was my mother's advice to her sons;
to study hard and follow your passions. (Philip)

Hang on tightly to faith, for it will be
the needed calm in life's torrential sea. (Rob)

I miss you so much more than you'll ever know.
But so glad you visit me in my dreams, though. (Susan)

If you go to bed every night at nine,
you'll wake up in the morning feeling fine. (Elaine)

Drink this vinegar with honey so sweet,
and by tomorrow your throat will feel neat. (Caleb)

If anyone in need came to our door,
my mother said to assist them for sure. (Brenda)

Mom would yell at us to keep the house warm,
Shut the door, you weren't born in a barn. (Mary Lee)

In these ways and more, our mothers were wise.
We are wise, too, if we take their advice. (Faith)

Celebrating America's Birthday   (written 6-28-21)

Each year we celebrate our country's birth.
Some say it is the greatest one on Earth. (Faith)

Saluting veterans is my fave way
To celebrate our Independence Day (Susan)

The 4th of July shows that we are one
That sacrifice allows us to have fun (Mary Lee)

Our country's flag with stripes of red and white
Flies in the breeze with its stars shining bright. (Barbara)

All those who have given their souls to Fate
Have given us this right to celebrate. (Robert)

A day to give thanks and praise
For service that our military gave (Elaine)

Freedom is not free is what we have heard
Be grateful for our freedom; let's pass the word! (Betty)

At memorials, make contemplation
Of sacrifices for our great nation. (Philip)

So join your kin, and proudly hang your flag
Make sure it is respectable, not a rag! (Brenda)

Salute the flag when a parade passes by
Beauty and meaning bring tears to my eyes. (Joan)

July 4th has plenty of fireworks
Thanks to God for our American perks. (Patty)

Prayers sent to the Lord for those fallen few
For whose blood was shed for me and for you. (Caleb)

Imperfect she may be in some folks' view
But, America, I love, cheer, and pray for you. (Mary Beth)

Summertime, 2021   (written 8-9-21)

Summertime! Season of colored pastels
Chatoyant panoramas grace the air   (Judy)

April showers are deluges daily
The ARK is now waiting for us to board (Mary Lee)

The full moon tickles the water with light
while lights from shrimp boats wink in the distance (Brenda)

On a summer stroll at a moonlit beach,
Salty waves splash upon a sandy shore. (Barbara)

Summer ushers in endless heat and rain,
and rainbows to light up the darkened sky. (Elaine)

Mississippi Sound Blue Crabs, hot and spicy;
Ice-cold watermelons drip with sweet juice.   (Betty)

Late summer daylight gives children a plus
And they drain every moment of playtime.   (Mary Beth)

Children in pool scream and splash with delight
On her float, tan Mama sips her julep. (Philip)

Sweet nighttime on the sandy shore, the breeze
Blows peace, tranquility into the soul. (Robert)

Summer vacations that aren't virtual
So welcome after the long quarantine. (Patty)

Couples walking hand in hand on the beach.
Kids with ice cream cones and cotton candy. (Joan)

The gardens now bring forth their production
Tomato sandwiches now fill bellies. (Caleb)

Summertime pleasures us each passing year.
A cyclical miracle like the moon. (Faith)

It's Fall Y'all   (written 10-4-21)

Fall is really here! And how do we know?
The temperature has fallen quite low!   (Brenda)

While we anticipate the first frost,
We remember the bountiful blooms now lost.   (Betty)

Tree leaves turn yellow, red, orange and brown
Soon after that, they just keep falling down.   (Barbara)

I don't have to mow the grass anymore
Now crack open a beer, don't be a bore.   (Caleb)

Winds of Fall arrive stirring memories
Of pumpkins and turkeys and Christmas trees. (Elaine)

Wonderful weather means sweaters and jeans
Holidays soon starting with Halloween. (Faith)

Fall's my very favorite time of year
Hayrides, wiener roasts are memories dear. (Joan)

68

Autumn leaves, cool winds, Friday night football
Homecoming dance, decorating the hall. (Judy)

The warmth of a fire, the snapping of flames,
The drums punctuating the team's football games. (Mary Beth)

Fall is the season we need to decrease,
And wait on the Savior to bring us peace. (Mary Lee)

October yields an abundant harvest
And the full moon smiles, 'You are truly blessed.' (Patty)

Goblins and witches, run on little feet
Ring doorbells and shout, "Hello! Trick or Treat!" (Philip)

As leaves are falling slowly to the ground
In peaceful solitude and silent sound. (Robert)

Now Thanksgiving is drawing ever near.
So let us ring it in with lots of cheer. (Susan)

Awesome Autumn   (written 11-30-21)

The falling leaves of orange, red, and gold
Herald in the arrival of winter's cold. (Elaine)

The cooling briskness of the early morn
Where body, soul and strength are now reborn. (Mary Lee)

Peter Anderson Festival - full swing
Many an item bought as gifts with bling (Susan)

Farewell to baseball and walk off home-runs.
We're cheering our football team on now for fun. (Mary Beth)

Changing seasons, falling leaves, hints of snow
Remind us Turkey Day is soon we know . (Joan)

The Myrtles spread their seeds upon the ground,
 Crunching faded flowers new life soon found. (Caleb)

The festive bird sits in all its array
Fam'lies gather to share Thanksgiving Day. (Judy)

The crisp air overtakes the weather now
And rests tranquility upon our brow. (Robert)

We thank the Lord for all of our blessings.
Then, tackle the turkey, gravy, dressings. (Brenda)

Days shorten, nights prolong,
We give our thanks in prayer and song. (Philip)

As nature tells the leaves it's time to go,
I pray I'll meet death with the grace they show. (Patty)

Awed by the beauty of glorious Fall,
We ponder God's blessings both great and small. (Faith)

We value this Fall with family and friends,
Being grateful for our faith that never ends. (Betty)

Soon autumn's grandeur will come to a close,
And cold winter's chill will nip at our nose. (Barbara)

Mississippi Poetry Society - South Branch
Poets of the Year

1988 - Eunice Davis Barnes of Pascagoula
1989 - Nina Parker Mason of Pascagoula
1990 - Beverly Corben (Brenda B. Finnegan received the
    Challenge Award)
1991 - Brenda Brown Finnegan of Pascagoula
1992 - Geneva Jo Anthony of Vancleave
1993 - Brenda Brown Finnegan (now living in Ocean
    Springs)
1994 - Monita Prine McLemore of Ocean Springs
1995 - Eunice Davis Barnes of Pascagoula
1996 - Monita Prine McLemore of Ocean Springs
1997 - Brenda Brown Finnegan of Ocean Springs
1998 - Geneva Jo Anthony of Vancleave
1999 - Helen J. Jarvis of Pascagoula
2000 - Geneva Jo Anthony of Vancleave
2001 - Helen J. Jarvis of Pascagoula
2002 - Elva Ware Avara of Pascagoula
2003 - Dorothy Rogers of Pascagoula
2004 - Nelda Broom of Pascagoula
2005 - Geneva Jo Anthony of Vancleave
2006 - Brenda Brown Finnegan of Ocean Springs
2007 - Patricia Butkovich of Gautier
2008 - Helen J. Jarvis of Pascagoula
2009 - Judy Davies of Gautier
2010 - Brenda Brown Finnegan of Ocean Springs
2011 - Patricia Butkovich of Gautier
2012 - Judy Davies of Gautier
2013 - none
2014 - none

2015 - Judy Davies of Gautier
2016 - Brenda Brown Finnegan of Ocean Springs
2017 - Judy S. Davies of Gautier
2018 - Brenda Brown Finnegan of Ocean Springs
2019 - none (Pandemic)
2020 - none (Pandemic)
2021 - Mary Lee Terry of Ocean Springs

Former members of MPS South Branch

We honor these past members of our group, some of whom are represented within this celebration as a remembrance of how much they meant to us. Our lives are richer for having known them.

Deceased:
Elva Avara 20 years (b. 11/19/35 - d. July 27, 2020).
Helen Jarvis 20 years (b. 6/20/28 - d. April 1, 2020)
Eunice Barnes* 20 years+
Voncile Ros 20 years + (b. 3/20/32 - d. 8/24/15)
James Atchley
Charles "Chuck" Gates
Dr. Hebert Corben*
Beverly Corben*
Roberta Powalski* 1st president of South Branch in 1982
Mildred Henderson
Sue Wright Entrekin*
Nina L. Mason
Frank J. Hasenhuettll*. (Was a poetry lover; but did not write)
Joseph E. Gould
Marguerite Watkins
Rev. John Ralph
Marian Eisensmith
Lola M. Douglas-Howard

Others:
Dorothy Rogers. (long time member - still active)
Carol Tucker
Cecile B. Clement*
Mildred Henderson*
Sheila Grieco *
W. Michiel Hawkins

Moved or no longer active:
Sheila Grieco (moved)
Mary C. Osterman (moved)
Barbara Moss (moved)
Dr. Gilbert Mason (deceased - was not active)
Monita McLemore (moved)

Faith Garbin (not active)
Robert Harkins (not active)
Betty L. Kempton
Becca Merritt
Louise W. Rogers
Felis Bouree
Norma H. Brown

Mississippi Poetry Society History
Established 1932
affiliated with the National Federation of State Poetry Societies

Mississippi Poetry Society, Inc. was founded in 1932 with eleven charter members at Belhaven College in Jackson and was first called Belhaven Poetry Society. Miss Elizabeth Newman, head of the English Department at Belhaven, was the first (honorary) president. Its stated objectives were: "to make citizens' poetry conscious, to awaken in young people the desire to write poetry, to collect and preserve in anthologies the best poetry produced in Mississippi, and to bring it to the attention of readers outside our own borders." The first elected president was Anne-Elise Roane Winter, who designed the MPS emblem, a shield with three silver stars on a dark blue vaulted sky, bearing the Latin phrase, "Ad Astra," (toward the stars). The first meetings were held in the Municipal Art Gallery in Jackson. William Alexander Percy of Greenville, cousin and adoptive father of Walker Percy, was an early member.

In 1935, MPS published its first anthology, *Singing Mississippi.* A second anthology, *Toward the Stars,* was published in 1944. In 1954, MPS held its first state-wide poetry festival in Hattiesburg. MPS was chartered by the State of Mississippi on May 9, 1957. Membership continued to grow, with monthly meetings in Jackson.

In 1957, MPS published *The Mississippi Poetry Journal,* marking the 25th anniversary of the Society. In October 1959, Goldie Jane Feldman of Jackson represented MPS at the organizational meeting of the **National Federation of State Poetry Societies (NSFPS)** in Baton Rouge, Louisiana, and Mississippi became a charter member of that group. In 1970, MPS began sponsoring a category in the NSFPS contest.

The first three Mississippi Poet Laureates were MPS members. Mrs. E. R. Prenshaw was Mississippi's Poet Laureate for 12 years, from 1961-1973. Governor Bill Waller appointed member Louise Moss Montgomery as Poet Laureate in 1973. Member Dr. Winifred Hamrick Farrar of Meridian was appointed as Poet Laureate in 1978 by Governor Cliff Finch, until her death in 2010. The 2012 Poet Laureate was Natasha Trethewey, a native Mississippian, now living in Atlanta, appointed to a 4-year term by Governor Haley Barbour. The Gulfport native won the 2007 Pulitzer Prize in poetry for her 2006 collection *Native Guard*. On June 7, 2012, James Billington, the Librarian of Congress, named her the 19th US Poet Laureate. On April 15, 2021, Governor Tate Reeves selected Catherine Pierce to serve a four-year term as Mississippi's Poet Laureate.

As early as 1953, discussion took place concerning establishing chapters so members could meet closer to their own homes, but the formal development of the branches did not happen until the 1980's, when three separate branches were established: the North Branch, established in 1980 in Aberdeen, the South Branch in Biloxi, in 1982, and the Central Branch, in Jackson, in 1987.

In 1982, the 50th anniversary anthology, *Lyric Mississippi* was published, and in 1992, MPS published a 60th anniversary anthology entitled, *Mississippi Melodies*. MPS was pleased to host the **National Federation of State Poetry Societies** in Biloxi in 1997. A collection of poems by the members, *Mississippi Musings,* was published that year. A 70th anthology, *Magnolia Heart-Songs* was published in

2002. The 75th anthology, *Mississippi Gems* was published in 2007, and our 80th anniversary anthology, *Mississippi Milestones,* was published in 2012. The 2017 anthology was entitled *Celebrating Mississippi* in honor of State of Mississippi's Bicentennial.

The history of MPS was lovingly kept for many years by Charlene Vetter Barr of Jackson. With the collaboration of Nina Mason of Pascagoula, her collection led to the publication in 1995 of the *History of the Mississippi Poetry Society, 1932-1995.* Early records are now housed in the Mississippi State Archives and History in Jackson.

The *Magnolia Muse* is the official newsletter of MPS, Inc. MPS' branches (now up to four branches) meet annually at a two-day Spring Festival, rotating locations around the state. Annual contest journals of winning poetry are published; The *Mississippi Poetry Journal* for adults while a separate journal is published for student winners. Dr. Emory D. Jones of Iuka was contest chairman and editor of the journals for several years. The current contest chairman is Steven Curry, assisted by out-going chairman, Jeanne S. Kelly, and Daniel Pickett. In keeping with current technology, MPS has a web site (www.misspoetry.net) as well as a Facebook page.

In 2001, MPS established a **Poet of the Year** competition for its members. An independent judge makes the final selection from the submissions, and the award includes publication of a chapbook and 25 copies to the winner. The first winner of the Poet of the Year competition was South Branch's own Brenda Brown Finnegan of Ocean Springs, who also won in 2020, during the pandemic. Her book, *Horn Island Vista* was finally debuted in Natchez in October 2021.

Our members have different levels of expertise, and those more experienced poets are happy to share their knowledge with new members.

We encourage students with no-fee categories in our annual contests. Our latest project is to obtain corporate support for our student categories. Student attendance was overwhelming at our 2019 Spring Festival in Jackson, and a ***Rising Stars Journal*** was published with their winning poems. All the 2020 activities were cancelled due to the Covid-19 pandemic, but our 2022 Spring Festival was held at Lake Tiak O'Khata in Louisville, MS.

A 501(c)3 nonprofit organization, MPS relies on grants to help pay for our annual speakers and to assist with attendance to the National Federation of State Poetry Societies conventions.

For the latest news, visit the Mississippi Poetry Society webpage at www.misspoetry.net/.

Submitted by Brenda B. Finnegan, South Branch Secretary
Ocean Springs, MS